A Rockpool book
PO Box 252
Summer Hill
NSW 2130
Australia

rockpoolpublishing.co
Follow us! **f** ⓘ rockpoolpublishing
Tag your images with #rockpoolpublishing

ISBN: 9781925946444
Northern Hemisphere Edition

Published in 2021 by Rockpool Publishing
Copyright text © Flavia Kate Peters and Barbara Meiklejohn-Free 2021
Copyright images © Nata Vedana 2021, featured on pages IV, V, XV, XXII, 5,
13, 19, 35, 36, 38, 48, 51, 67, 73, 80, 82, 89, 90, 104, 105, 108, 110, 116,
117, 122, 125, 127, 138, back cover and inside front jacket.
All other images by Shutterstock.

Cover and Text Design by Dana Brown, Rockpool Publishing
Edited by Jody Lee
Typeset by Liz Seymour

Printed and bound in China
10 9 8 7 6 5 4 3 2 1

RECLAIMING THE MAGICK OF THE OLD WAYS

2022 WITCH'S DIARY

NORTHERN HEMISPHERE

FLAVIA KATE PETERS   BARBARA MEIKLEJOHN-FREE

ROCKPOOL

PIONEERS OF THE CRAFT

The Witch's Diary honours all those who have given their lives to the Craft. They are the founders, wisdom keepers, elders and leaders who have gone before us, who have ensured that we today hold the sacred knowledge of the ancients, despite the gruesome punishments many faced and still face today in mainstream society and particular cultures for their beliefs.

Let us remember those seen and unseen, known and unknown and give our undying gratitude to all those who have shone the light of magick through the darkness.

Today we witches stand side by side, strong in our beliefs, whilst the ancestors walk beside us, and we are proud to call ourselves WITCHES OF THE CRAFT.

So Mote it be.

Hail and Welcome!

The *2022 Witch's Diary* is a magickal tool in which you can draw upon ancient wisdom, and is relevant to the modern witch today, enabling one to thrive in balance and harmony – with a sprinkle of very real magick, in conjunction with the witches' wisdom of old.

The truth is that witches are everywhere. A witch is someone just like you, who has always been drawn to nature, who naturally hears the whispers of the ancestors through the breeze, who welcomes the rains, glorifies in the heat of the sun and connects with the nourishment of the earth. A witch embraces each season, rejoices at every new bud during the first stirrings of Spring, the harvest abundance that Summer supplies, the falling leaves of Autumn and revels in the deep, dark mystery that accompanies the Winter months.

A witch's heart sings at the mere notion of magick, has an affinity with the ways of natural healing and believes in another world of mystical beings. The natural witch is able to connect with this 'other' world, perceiving and working in conjunction with the ancestors whose wisdom and guidance can be drawn from. This is the way of the witch. A witch is a healer who embraces the workings of nature, and takes a responsible attitude in guardianship for our beloved planet, and those who reside on it.

Now more than ever, you are being urged to awaken the witch within and integrate with the magick and mystery of yesteryear. As you walk along the ancient path of the witch and as an advocate of the Old Ways you will find freedom to express who you truly are and reclaim your personal power as you harness the magick of nature and the innate powers of witches' wisdom.

The Witch's Diary is ideal for anyone who has a love for nature, who wishes to bring the magick of the Old Ways into their everyday lives. Each month you will discover how to work with specific moon phases and weekdays in order to harness your personal power and enhance your magickal abilities.

Journey through the year as you work with the forces of nature through spell work, incantations, recipes, herbs, and much more.

This diary is perfect for both the seasoned witch and for those who are exploring the ancient path of the wise. Each page is a magickal avenue to draw upon ancient wisdom that is still relevant for the modern witch today.

You'll find each page assists you well,
Through incantation, message, spell.
Tools explained, history unearthed.
Allowing magick to be birthed.
The witch in you will be empowered
No more will others leave you soured
Look no further than inside.
It's here the magick doth reside.

Blessed Be,
Flavia and Barbara

MOON PHASES

~ Dark or Old ~

Powerful time to banish, remove things,
people or situations. A time to neutralise
spells made against others. Powerful times
for understanding fears and anger.
Also good for bringing about justice.

*Time of transition from the
Dark Moon to the New Moon.

~ Waxing Crescent ~

Constructive magick, to increase things.
New beginnings, new relationships, best time
to set intentions, to focus intention for positive
outcomes. Sowing of seeds for new ventures.
Projects coming to life.

~ First Quarter Moon ~

Best time to draw things in, such as money,
success, friends, lovers, work. Attracting that
which you most desire into manifestation. Also
a good time for house hunting or finding lost
objects. Time of acceleration and growth.

~ Waxing Gibbous ~

For renewal of strength and energy. Time to
focus on willpower and seeing things through.
Time to surrender to the universe and trust.
This is the most powerful time of the moon
for fruition and completion.

~ Full ~

Releases what no longer serves. Full Moon removes old habits and other issues. This is a time to harness extra power to get over difficult challenges. Rituals and spells for protection, divination, and for healing of longstanding illness. This is the time of manifestation and empowerment. The full moon is most powerful and its magick is potent.

~ Waning Gibbous ~

Great time to expel all negative thoughts and influences. Waning moon energies rid and repel. A time to decrease, to bring to an end. A time of facing shadows.

~ Last Quarter ~

A time of transitions and change, to avoid temptations. A remover of obstacles.

~ Waning Crescent ~

Banishment, retreat. A healing of transition between the death of the old and the birth of the New Moon.

Between the Dark and the Waxing Crescent is a period of stillness called the New Moon, which is the space between the past and new beginnings. This is a very powerful phase of transition.

LUNAR AND SOLAR ECLIPSES

Eclipses are magickal astrological events that can fuel a witch's intentions, wishes and spells with cosmic energy to manifest new beginnings and empower positive change.

A solar eclipse occurs during a New Moon. When the sun, moon and earth are in alignment the moon casts a shadow across the Earth which blocks out the sun, fully or partially. For witches, the solar eclipse means harnessing the magick of new beginnings, to truly transform.

A lunar eclipse occurs only during a Full Moon. When the sun and earth are in close alignment with the moon, it moves into the Earth's shadow and becomes obscured, fully or partially. For witches, the Lunar eclipse means harnessing the magick of empowerment and manifestation.

2022

30 April **Solar Eclipse** (partial)

15–16 May **Lunar Eclipse** (total)

25 October **Solar Eclipse** (partial)

8 November **Lunar Eclipse** (total)

2023

20 April 20 **Solar Eclipse** (total)

5–6 May **Lunar Eclipse** (penumbral)

14 October **Solar Eclipse** (annular – ring of fire)

28–29 October **Lunar Eclipse** (partial)

FULL MOONS

January ~ Olde, Frost, Birch, Cold Moon.
Letting go of the past, invoking the new.

February ~ Ice, Snow, Rowen, Quicking Moon.
The journey of the soul inwards.

March ~ Moon of Winds, Storm, Ash, Worm, Crow Moon.
Coming from the darkness to the light.

April ~ Growing, Alder, Seed Moon.
Growth and planting of new ideas.

May ~ Hare, Milk, Bright, Willow Moon.
Attention to your needs and of those you love.

June ~ Moon of Horses, Hawthorn, Strawberry Moon.
Balance and understanding.

July ~ Hay, Thunder, Mead, Oak Moon.
Making plans for the future.

August ~ Corn, Holly, Grain Moon.
Removing excess baggage, being flexible.

September ~ Harvest, Hazel, Fruit, Barley Moon.
Completion and future prospects.

October ~ Blood, Vine, Hunters Moon.
Soul growth and deep wisdom within.

November ~ Snow, Ivy, Dark Moon.
Truth and honesty, reassessing your life.

December ~ Wolf, Elder, Cold Moon.
Healing old wounds and emotions.

WHEEL OF THE YEAR

Spiritual wisdom can be gained by recognising the traditions of old witchcraft and the connection to the seasons. As the witches of old worked with the elemental forces of nature, they also honoured the aspects of the Triple Goddess, in relation to the seasons and festivals celebrated through the Wheel of the Year.

In nature the year is made up of four seasons. It is the Sun that marks any seasonal change and these changes are honoured by celebrating four Solar Festivals. Fire Festivals are marked by cross quarter and equinox celebrations, and so all together eight festivals of the seasons become the Wheel of the Year. These festivals represent the state of nature at the time, the agricultural calendar and the physical and spiritual effects the time of year has on human-kind.

From planting in the Spring, to harvesting in Autumn, the seasons are of great importance. Different celebrations mark times to count our blessings, for reaping and recognising all that we've sowed and for giving thanks to the nature spirits, as well as to Goddess (in her Triple aspect of Maiden, Mother, Crone), who continues the circle that we call life on Earth.

CROSS-QUARTER FESTIVALS AND EQUINOXES

IMBOLC ~ 1 February

This is a time of new growth, as new shoots appear from the ground, early shoots begin to show and so we begin to witness the start of the renewal of life. The Maiden; innocence, purity, seeding the dream and birthing the inner child.

OSTARA ~ 21-22 March

When balance hangs in the air and the length of day equals that of night when we celebrate the birth of new life. The Maiden matures; from dark to light we explore signs of growth and discernment.

BELTANE ~ 1 May

A fire festival to celebrate the full bloom of nature. The Mother; fertile minds, bodies and souls, birthing our ideas and soul's knowing.

LITHA ~ 21-22 June

Celebrations of Summer Solstice, the longest day of the year. The Mother glorified; celebration of light, being in our full glory.

LAMMAS ~ 1 August

When the grain harvest is cut down and celebrated. The Mother matures; gratitude for earthly, physical sustenance.

MABON ~ 21-22 September

When day and night is balanced and the fruit harvest is celebrated. The Crone; the art of contemplation explored, self-sufficiency of mind, body and spirit.

SAMHAIN ~ 31st October

An honouring of the souls of the dead, when the veil between the worlds are thinnest. The Crone revered; respecting our ancestors, healing our hurts.

YULE ~ 21-22 December

Winter Solstice is a celebration of the rebirth of the sun, for now that the longest night is here the days start to grow longer hereafter. The Crone fades; the returning sun, exploring purest energy the essence of our being.

PLANTING AND HARVESTING DAYS

Witches have always planted according to the moon cycles and in conjunction with the movement of the planets. They understood that different plants grow better when they are planted during different phases of the moon. Each of these phases imparts an influence on the way vegetation grows on the planet through the rising and falling of the moisture in the ground and in the plants. But it's not just planting that is the most important time for the farmer as harvest time also has to be considered. Harvesting at the correct time ensures crops last much longer. It is down to how the plant stores the water in the fruit/crop at different times of the moon cycle.

~ NEW MOON ~
An excellent time to sow leafy plants like cabbages, broccoli, celery and cauliflower, and to transplant leafy annuals.

~ WAXING MOON ~
Sap flows and rises, a good time for new growth.
Sow or transplant flowering annuals, biennials and grains.
Plant fruits or flowers that are to be harvested.

~ FIRST QUARTER ~
A time to plant tomatoes, beets, broccoli,
beans and squashes.

~ FULL MOON ~
A time to sow or plant root crops like potatoes and asparagus and fruit perennials, such as apples and rhubarb.
Perfect for separating plants and for taking cuttings.

~ WANING MOON ~
Sap is drawn down. Plant perennials and root crops.
A good time to prune and harvest.

~ LAST QUARTER ~
A time to weed, dig or plough and to improve
the soil with compost or manure.

PLANET RULERS AND SIGNS

Aries ~ Mars

Taurus ~ Venus

Gemini ~ Mercury

Cancer ~ Moon

Leo ~ Sun

Virgo ~ Mercury

Libra ~ Venus

Scorpio ~ Mars

Sagittarius ~ Jupiter

Capricorn ~ Saturn

Aquarius ~ Uranus

Pisces ~ Neptune

THE GODDESS
AND MOON PHASES

The Goddess was worshipped in conjunction with the phases of the moon: waxing, full and waning phases which represented the three phases of the Goddess as Maiden, Mother and Crone.

MAIDEN

ASPECTS ~ Beauty, enchantment, inception, expansion, new beginnings, youth, excitement, virgin, innocence

Season: Spring
Colour: White
Moon Phase: Waxing

FESTIVAL ~ Imbolc, Ostara (Spring Equinox)

MOTHER

ASPECTS ~ Ripeness, fertility, growth, fulfilment, stability, giving, nurturing, compassionate

Season: Summer
Colour: Red
Moon Phase: Full

FESTIVAL ~ Beltane, Litha (Summer Solstice), Mabon (Autumn Equinox)

CRONE

ASPECTS ~ Wisdom, repose, magick, destruction, decay and death

Season: Winter
Colour: Black
Moon Phase: Waning/Dark or New

FESTIVAL ~ Samhain (Hallowe'en), Yule (Winter Solstice)

MAGICKAL WEEKDAYS

Sunday

Day of the god Apollo, ruled by the Sun. This day is imbued with energy and divine guidance. A perfect day to relax, unwind and focus on health and wellbeing to light up one's inner sunshine.

Monday

Day of the goddess Diana, ruled by the moon. This is a day for discovering one's true potential and intuition. Looking deep within and honouring emotions.

Tuesday

Day of Týr, ruled by Mars. A day of projects and decision making, new jobs. To fulfil dreams, goals and desires.

Wednesday

Day of the god Woden (Odin) ruled by Mercury. A day of expressing oneself and focus on life decisions. A time for communication and messages.

Thursday

Day of the god Thor, ruled by Jupiter. A day of gratitude and positivity. A time of expansion of the mind, body and spirit.

Friday

Day of the goddess Frige, ruled by Venus. A day of love and self-care. A time to create and connect with others.

Saturday

Day of Saturn. Time to be grounded and balanced. Great day to tackle big projects, of being responsible and getting organised both at home and at work.

MAGICKAL MOON TIMES TO CAST SPELLS

Dark Moon ~ From dawn to sunset.

Waxing Crescent ~ From mid-morning to after sunset.

First Quarter ~ From noon until midnight.

Waxing Gibbous ~ From mid-afternoon until 3 am.

Full Moon ~ From sunset to dawn.

Waning Gibbous ~ Mid-evening until mid-morning.

Last Quarter Moon ~ From midnight until noon.

Waning Crescent Moon ~ From 3 am until mid-afternoon.

MAGICKAL MEANINGS OF COLOURS

WHITE ~ Purification, blessings, aspect of light, cosmos

BLACK ~ Elimination, banishment, retribution, North, Earth

BLUE ~ Peace, harmony, healing, curing fevers, re-uniting friendships, house blessings

BROWN ~ Grounding, stabilising, intuition, balance, connection to Mother Earth

GOLD ~ Cosmic influences, solar dieties, success, wealth, influence

GREEN ~ Fertility, good fortune, generosity, wealth, success, renewal, marriage, healing

INDIGO ~ Meditation, balancing Karma, stopping gossip and astral projection

MAGENTA ~ Rapid change, spiritual healing and exorcism

ORANGE ~ Communication, telepathy, new job, adaptability, luck, control, attraction

PINK ~ Romance, affection, love, spiritual awakening, unity

PURPLE ~ Honour, respect, wisdom, Divine knowing, trust and spiritual connection

SILVER ~ Moon magick, protection from entities, inner peace, serenity

MAGICKAL DIRECTIONS AND ELEMENTS

NORTH ~ Element of Earth. Season of Winter. Time of the New Moon and midnight.

EAST ~ Element of Air. Season of Spring. Time of the waxing moon and sunrise.

SOUTH ~ Element of Fire. Season of Summer. Time of the Full Moon and noon.

WEST ~ Element of Water. Season of Autumn. Time of the waning moon and dusk.

ABOVE ~ Mind connection with the Universal Great Mystery .

BELOW ~ Body connection with the Earth

WITHIN ~ Spirit connection with one's inner universe, the Great Void.

TREE
MAGICKAL PROPERTIES

ALDER ~ Resurrection, rebirth and fire.

APPLE ~ Healing, prosperity, love, peace, happiness and youth.

ASH ~ Healing, protection and sea magick.

BLACKTHORN ~ Bad luck, strife, unexpected changes, death, wounding and curses.

BIRCH ~ New beginnings and births, fertility, purifications, protection and blessings.

CEDAR ~ Purification, prosperity, and longevity. Represents earth, spirituality.

ELDER ~ Healing, love, protection and prosperity. Used to make magickal wands.

ELM ~ Primordial female powers and protection.

FIR ~ Youth and vitality. Used in prosperity magick.

HAWTHORN ~ Female sexuality, cleansing, marriage, love and protection. Magickal tool.

HAZEL ~ Fertility, divination, marriage, protection, and reconciliation, wands.

HOLLY ~ Protection.

OAK ~ Healing, strength and longevity.

PINE ~ Immortality, fertility, health, prosperity and represents earth.

ROWAN ~ Protection, healing and strength. Represents fire.

WILLOW ~ Moon and wishing magick, healing, protection, enchantments. Represents water.

YEW ~ Immortality, rebirth, protection, longevity, change, divinity, strength.

TREE INCANTATION

Standing tall, often ignored
Branches cut down, chopped and sawed
Witches scream out and cry
'Stop your wrath, this tree will die!'
Time to seek the truth it weaves
Magick, wisdom, found in leaves
So heal beneath an Oak or Yew
Its energies will sustain you.

2022
WITCH'S
DIARY

MONTHS

NEW YEAR SPELL

Take a piece of material from whatever or whomever
is preventing you from moving forward. Place a bowl
of water in front of you, and under a waning moon and say:

The door is closing to the past
For future's sake, it couldn't last
The worst is gone, prepare for change
Letting go may feel strange
The door is closed, won't look back
New year ahead, back on track
Release old ties, to set me free
Material holds past energy
Submerge in water, hold it down
Allow the past to fully drown
Gratitude for lesson learned
New door opens, truly earned

Show the bowl the door by placing it outside until the Dark Moon.

So mote it be.

28 Tuesday

29 Wednesday

30 Thursday

31 Friday

1 Saturday
Janet Horne was the last woman in the United Kingdom to be executed legally in 1727.

2 Sunday
New Moon.

JANUARY

Olde, Frost, Birch and Cold Moon

Letting go of the past, invoking the new

January brings us the energy of a new start as the calendar year begins. In the Northern Hemisphere the cold, hard earth remains steeped in deep magick and mystery, nurturing and restoring all that reside within it, offering comfort from the hardships and discomfort that the glacial callousness of Winter brings. The Goddess is in her Crone phase, but now she is beginning to fade as the promise of new life beckons and the days are getting longer, since her deathly reign of Winter and the Solstice at Yule. Now is the time of slow awakening for all of nature, and to look at new goals as we leave old regrets behind and make new resolutions through intention, ritual and spells, to assist us through the months of the long year that now awaits.

It is time to take the first brave steps of authenticity towards the magickal freedom of embracing the witch within, to stop hesitating and hiding in the shadows. Bid farewell to negativity, control and disempowerment and embrace the lessons of the past, as the door closes on yesteryear and brighter experiences await. The Crone offers you rebirth and transformation as you follow the Wheel of the Year and the magick of the Old Ways.

GODDESS: Danu (Celtic/Irish), First Great Mother, Earth Goddess, Cosmic Triple Goddess

CRONE: Transformation, dreams, clarity, wisdom, alchemical magick

WITCH'S FAMILIAR

SNAKE - Difficulties in letting go of the past is my invitation to slither into your life to bring about major change. For I know that if you don't shed your old skin you will perish and die within. Past thoughts and feelings that keep rearing their ugly head will strike out at you, as well as others, without warning. The illusions of the past are controlling your abilities to see clearly and you have become blinded to the immense healing opportunities I offer, of shedding what no longer serves your higher purpose to bring about a metamorphosis to change and new beginnings. From this place of transition you are more able to tap into my wisdom to decipher when is the right time to strike out. Be watchful of biting reactions as you outgrow the old. As rebirth takes place, my antidote will diffuse both your poisoned thoughts and complications. I will clear the way so you can take the path of least resistance to new life that awaits you now.

SNAKE ~ REBIRTH

Tendencies to strike out and bite
Shed the past, t'was yesterday's fight
Transmute the old, and seek to evolve
Transitional change rebirths one's resolve

MAGICK RITUAL

Hold a cleansed piece of clear quartz crystal upon
your Third Eye chakra. Imagine a golden light streaming
through the crystal, clearing away blockages, awakening
your spiritual sight to bring about visions and clarity.
Time to dream your dreams awake.

ROSEMARY ~ MEMORIES

Delve into the distant past
Memories made, meant to last
I'll raise vibes from lethargy
And purify your energy
This magick is worked, with harm to none.
So mote it be. There, it is done

3   Monday

4   Tuesday
Doreen Valiente, (1922–1999), Mother of modern witchcraft, United Kingdom.

5   Wednesday
Barbara Meiklejohn-Free, (1957–), High Priestess, Highland Seer, Occultist, United Kingdom.

6   Thursday

7   Friday

8   Saturday
Samuel Liddell MacGregor Mathers (1854-1918). One of the founders of the Golden Dawn, United Kingdom.

9   Sunday
First Quarter Moon.

10 **Monday**

---

11 **Tuesday**

Trial of the Basque witches began in January of 1609, Logrono, Spain.

---

12 **Wednesday**

---

13 **Thursday**

---

14 **Friday**

KITCHEN WITCHERY

ROSEMARY - Echoes of your distant past sound all around when you find me growing nearby. Remembering the good times and those special moments remind you of who you have been, and how far you have come. Messages from long ago evoke sweet recollections that play out as visions in your imagination and embrace your heart with warm feelings of memorable love. However, old memories that haunt your dreams and invade your thoughts remind you of the darker times you'd rather forget. Hold me in meditation or spend time with me in the kitchen, for my purification properties will dislodge the heavy and unpleasant energies that have been hanging around of late. Use the cleansing smoke of my dried leaves or add a strong infusion to the bath to banish toxic vibes, for I am a powerful energetic purifier. The magick of how you once felt will return as you transcend forward into your destiny.

15 Saturday

16 Sunday

WITCHY RECIPE

Hair tonic for the loss of hair, baldness, healthy scalp

Take four stalks of fresh rosemary, strip the leaves off and chop
up finely. Fill a saucepan with 3 cups of spring or filtered water,
add the rosemary, cover with a lid and boil for 30 minutes.
Steep for 30 minutes then strain the mixture. Add this to your 3 cups
of homemade apple cider (see September's recipe
on page 101) and shake. Label hair tonic.

---

17   Monday

Full Moon.

18 Tuesday

19 Wednesday
Valais, Switzerland (1428–1447), 367 people condemned for witchcraft.

20 Thursday

21 Friday

22 Saturday
Tier, Germany (1581–1593), 368 people condemned for witchcraft.

23 Sunday

24 Monday
Theoris of Lemnos (4th century BC), Greek Witch, Folk Healer. Executed.

25 Tuesday
Third Quarter Moon.

26 Wednesday

27 Thursday

28 Friday
Agnes Sampson (died 1591). Burnt as a witch. Royal Mile, Edinburgh.

---

29 Saturday

---

30 Sunday
Persecution of witches in Rome continued until late 4th century AD.

FEBRUARY

Ice, Snow, Rowen and Quicking Moon

A time of purification and hope

After the harshness of Winter, this is a time of emergence as new shoots appear from the ground, early flowers begin to blossom and so we begin to witness the start of the renewal of life. Daylight hours finally start to become noticeably longer at this time and we celebrate the birth of the very first lambs as the ewes start to lactate. It was an important time for our ancestors, as fresh milk once again became available, meaning the difference between life and death after the cold, harsh scarcity of Winter.

IMBOLC Northern Hemisphere: 1 February

GODDESS: Bridget (Irish/Celtic), new life, hope, growth

MAIDEN: Innocence, purity and seeding the dream

IMBOLC

First signs of new growth

Today, at Imbolc, it is still tradition to pour fresh milk on the ground to honour the Earth Mother and to ensure fertility for the coming season. For in agriculture this is when seeds are planted and we start to see signs of flowers starting to grow, such as snowdrops and crocuses in the Northern Hemisphere.

Imbolc is a time of purification in preparation for the coming year and is portrayed as the young virgin Maiden aspect of the Celtic Triple Goddess. She is the young girl awakening to womanhood just as nature begins its fertility cycle and offers us new life, new beginnings.

This is the time to seed your new ideas, to make plans and begin creative projects that will grow into fruition through the coming warmer months. Imbolc signifies new beginnings, for as nature starts to wake up it is a time to plant and seed your wishes and desires, to awaken and create new dreams and goals.

IMBOLC INCANTATION

'Neath a layer of soft white snow
Doth a single flower grow.
The Goddess stands in 'Maiden' form,
Shining through this very Dawn.
New fruits stir her virgin womb,
Awakening from Winter's tomb.
She calls to you to be free.
Explore each possibility.
For now is when to seed your dreams,
No matter how hard and tough life seems,
They will come true, it's time to trust.
Be one with nature, don't fight or thrust.
Take the cup she offers you,
That's filled with milk from an ewe.
Embrace the year through open eyes.
Magick awaits, nature tells no lies.

31   **Monday**

1   Tuesday

Imbolc · New Moon · Persecution of the Cathars in France (around 1450) for witchcraft and heresy.

2   Wednesday

3   Thursday

4   Friday

5   Saturday

6   Sunday

7   **Monday**

8   **Tuesday**

First Quarter Moon · Eliphas Levi Zahed, greatest Occultist of the nineteenth century.

9   **Wednesday**

10   **Thursday**

11   **Friday**

WITCH'S WISDOM

New opportunities present themselves as you become in tune with the cycles of nature. The ancient mystics worked with the cycle of nature and recognised that when we operate in this way we receive all that we need to survive abundantly. As you become aware of this awakening you will begin to notice synchronicities, your wishes and desires will powerfully evolve as you start to live as your authentic self. Imbolc opens new doorways for you and what no longer serves you will fall away naturally. There's a glimmer of hope sparkling in the distance, that indicates new ideas, beginnings and golden opportunity. This is an auspicious time as you awaken the true witch that lies within, and which now stirs from a deep slumber. So purify your thoughts, actions and diet for this is a time of new growth for you as you seed fresh ideas. Time to wake up!

12   Saturday

13   Sunday

---

14 Monday

---

15 Tuesday

---

16 Wednesday

Full Moon · Pamela Colman Smith (1878–1951), Occultist, Artist of the Rider-Waite Tarot.

---

17 Thursday

---

18 Friday

INCANTATION

The Goddess stands in 'Maiden' form,
Shining through this very Dawn.
New fruits stir in her virgin womb,
Awaken now from Winter's tomb.
This magick is worked, with harm to none.
So mote it be. There, it is done.

---

19   Saturday

---

20   Sunday

21   Monday

---

22   Tuesday

La Voisin (1640-1680), French Fortune-Teller, Sorceress and Commissioned Poisoner.
Burnt at the stake · Sybil Leek (1917-1982), Witch, Occult Author and Astrologer.

---

23   Wednesday

---

24   Thursday

---

25   Friday

Third Quarter Moon.

KITCHEN WITCHERY

SAGE – Stale energies can block magickal intentions and prevent desired outcomes. Time for a little spiritual Spring cleaning! Use the white variety in a cleansing ritual to smudge contaminants, and get your working space ceremonially clean. My power of purification will clear and lift the energy of your altar as you waft the smoke from a lit bundle over the sacred area. I will wipe the vibrational slate clean around your home to disassociate household items with their past vibrations, and lift them to match with a higher frequency.

My garden variation is well known as a culinary herb, for my aroma is both sweet and savoury and I'm used for countless kitchen witchery spells. For as well as promoting wisdom and building emotional strength, I also assist in manifestation magick, and bring you pure luck.

---

26 Saturday

---

27 Sunday
Comte de Saint Germain (1712–1784), Hungarian Alchemist and Philosopher.

WITCH'S TIP

Smudging and purification with sage has been used in ceremony for thousands of years. The protective energy of this sacred herb can be used to clear away and cleanse unwanted or negative energy. Light a stick of White Californian sage, softly blow out the flame and let the sage smoulder as it rests in a shell or dish. Use your hands to sweep the smoke up and around your body and auric field. You will feel cleansed, clear and so much lighter.

SAGE ~ PURIFICATION

Shrubby sage, sacred space
I'll purify and cleanse your place
Vibrations raised, no longer stuck
Assist, I shall, to bring you luck
This magick is worked, with harm to none.
So mote it be. There, it is done.

NEW HOPE SPELL

Write down your dreams and all you desire and put them in a
self-addressed envelope. Hold some hardy annual seeds, such as
calendula, during a waxing crescent moon, focus your intentions for
the future into the seeds and say:

Into seeds I place all hope
And pop them in an envelope
Send to future self, post-haste
Things to do, no time to waste.
Goals to set, dreams to sow.
A new door opens to walk through.

Post the envelope and plant the seeds, when received,
under a Full Moon for your dreams to grow into fruition.

MARCH

Moon of Winds, Storm, Ash, Worm and Crow Moon

Coming from the darkness growing into the light

In like a lion and out like a lamb, the winds of change welcome in this wild month which brings hope of warmer days to come. The energy at this waxing time of year becomes expansive as the light grows strong enough to defeat the dark, and the natural world comes alive as the Sun gains strength with the promise of longer and warmer days. As the goddess in her Maiden form walks across the land, all of nature wakes up to the fulfilled promises made at Imbolc, as she breathes new life into the world. Spring has sprung!

OSTARA Northern Hemisphere: 21 March

GODDESS: Eostre/Ostara (Anglo/Germanic)
of Spring, fertility, renewal and fruitfulness.

MAIDEN: The dark of the old aligns with new light,
signs of growth and creative power.

OSTARA

Alignment of the natural world

Ostara heralds the Spring Equinox. A time of balance between light and dark, a day of equilibrium. When we are aligned with the natural world we can embrace and honour the new creative power that is stirring throughout nature.

It is a time for honouring new life and is the festival that has been 'borrowed' from age old traditions, to become Easter. Think hatched eggs, baby chicks, moon gazy hares and all the fresh promises of Spring. Call upon the Spirits of the Air to enhance your creativity, meditation abilities and to stimulate your mind as you light incense, a yellow candle and face the direction of East. This is a great time for fertility as Air blows you in the direction of new beginnings. So throw caution to the wind and watch as your visions manifest into reality.

OSTARA INCANTATION

Celebrate the stirring of Spring.
Natural balance, doth it bring.
Claim that of which it represents;
New life, growth and expectance.
Seeds planted in nature's tomb,
Incubate within Her womb.
Symbolic hares upon the lawn
Herald the Goddess of the Dawn
And from the East the sun doth rise
Shining bright across the skies
The goddess works behind the scenes
To manifest your goals and dreams
Await and trust now. T'is the key.
For life will bloom most readily.

28 **Monday**

1 Tuesday
First Witchcraft Act in England in 1542. Instigator was Henry VIII.

2 Wednesday
New Moon.

3 Thursday

4 Friday

5 Saturday

6 Sunday
Laurie Cabot (1933–), Salem, United States, High Priestess and Occultist.

7   Monday

8   Tuesday

9   Wednesday

10   Thursday
First Quarter Moon.

11   Friday

12   Saturday
Hypatia (360AD- 415AD), ancient philosophy, astronomy. Murdered by a mob who accused her of witchcraft.

WITCH'S WISDOM

Like the sun rising at Spring Equinox, Ostara's promise of balance and fertility is on the horizon for you. You have all the necessary steps in order for what you want to happen to come about. But first you must allow everything to unfold naturally. The seeds planted at Imbolc need time to nurture deep within the Earth, and even though these seedlings may now be appearing, still you are yet to witness them grow into full bloom. So have patience, as this is a time of incubation, for the development of any projects, wishes, spells and dreams you have breathed energy into. Everything is simmering under the surface and the timing is perfect to bring the best results. That which you cannot see needs to take place first, in the background. So don't try to speed up the process, just wait, trust and allow the natural order of things to take place. All good things come to those who wait, and remember that great things come from small beginnings.

INCANTATION

Ostara takes you by the hand
As Spring awakens o'er the land
In magick wishes do come true.
Believe these things will come to you.
Now close your eyes, count up to three.
Trust in what you cannot see.

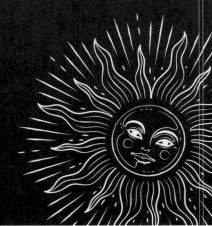

13   Sunday

KITCHEN GUIDANCE

EUCALYPTUS – Time to clear the air, for emotions have been stuffed down and feelings of being trapped and suffocated have restricted you. Allow me to bring you some welcome relief, to cleanse you both spiritually and physically, for it's time to breathe again. As I bring fresh energy to your situation and relieve you of any mental exhaustion, my high water content and calming properties gift you with purity and stimulation as I restore clarity to your recent over-active mind. Inhale my strong minty scent to open up your airwaves and expand your lungs, to enhance your creative pathways. I assist with respiratory issues too, so add a few drops to steam and breathe in deeply my antibacterial and antiseptic curative properties, which are strong enough to relieve asthma and sinus congestion. I will also expel any residual energies as you cleanse your ritual tools with oil, and as you burn my leaf I will escort all negative influences away.

EUCALYPTUS ~ BREATHE

Breathe me in, breathe me out
My pungent minty scent has clout
Relieves the body, clears the mind
Now take a breath and unwind
This magick is worked, with harm to none.
So mote it be. There, it is done.

14　Monday

15   Tuesday

16   Wednesday

17   Thursday

18   Friday
Full Moon · Manly Palmer Hall (1901-1990), Mystic and Astrologer.

19   Saturday

20   Sunday

21   Monday
Ostara (Spring Equinox).

22   Tuesday

23   Wednesday

24   Thursday

25   Friday
Third Quarter Moon.

WITCHY RECIPE

Eucalyptus oil: for decongestant, disinfectant, antiseptic, deodorant.

Take two dark mason jars and add half a cup of fresh leaves to one jar. Add a thin layer of sea salt and using a long spoon smash the leaves releasing their natural oils into the salt. Add 2 cups of an essential oil of your choiceand steep in the sunshine for at least 3 weeks. Remember to shake the jar every day. After 3 weeks or more strain into the second jar and store in a dark place or the fridge.

---

26 Saturday

Zhang Laing in 646 AD executed for treason and witchcraft.

---

27 Sunday

WITCH'S FAMILIAR

HARE – Your desire is for total change, where you can be true to yourself, let your guard down and take it easy. Call on my power now to help you achieve a new freedom, whether it's just a different way of thinking about things or a real-life transformation. I will help you seek out the people who can support you through this, to guide and advise. Follow my path and the options will present themselves to you along the way, but be sure to keep up, I seldom rest for long and this opportunity won't linger. A quick decision is needed, so get active for doing nothing is not an option.

HARE ~ NEW FREEDOM

Desire for change, and to improve
Things to amend, update, approve
Freedom awaits, time to declare
Restyle, transform, trust in the hare
Upon the air now blows a gust
Time to focus, believe and trust

FERTILITY SPELL

Face the direction of East at sunrise,
hold an egg in your hand and infuse it
with your ideas and plans, and say:

Facing East upon the dawn
Empower my fruitfulness this morn
Ideas conceived, growing strong
Pregnant wishes. Won't be long!
Crack the egg, pour on the earth
Fertile land assists the birth
Keep positive, forget all strife
New beginnings bring new life

APRIL

Growing, Alder and Seed Moon

Growth, planting and connecting with the magick of nature.

The fresh light rain of April, in the Northern Hemisphere, brings with it fresh ideas and inspiration. This is a great time for wishes and magick as the earth springs forth and faeries tend to and nurture their wards, the newly growing flowers. For thousands of years witches and healers have worked alongside the power of the Fae, who have shared ancient knowledge of healing herbs, cures and ointments with those who have visited their mystical world. As a new magickal energy of growth surrounds you, the faeries are poised to support you too, as any heartfelt wishes reflect your thoughts and good intentions. They are the magickal guardians of nature who remind you that magick is everywhere and in everything. Go outside and discover it! Enjoy every precious moment, knowing and appreciating that you are totally blessed as you feel the Faery Witch within stir deeply.

GODDESS: Cordelia (Celtic/British),
Faery Queen of flowers, faeries, beauty and wishes

MAIDEN: Renewing the spirit, inhaling fresh
air and the fragrance of Spring flowers

KITCHEN GUIDANCE

DANDELION – The wishes you have made are floating around in the ether. They will not come true until the very moment you believe that they will, for it is belief that is a key ingredient when it comes to making magick. Your obsession for possession has blinded you to unseen factors that are blocking the attainment of your goals. There is something that you want so strongly that nothing else matters. You must be clear about what you wish for and believe me when I say that everything is possible – even the impossible! When it comes to making magick, a little focus is required, as well as belief. When my flowers of bright yellow turn a mystical white, make your desires known into my seed head. Blow on me gently, to release your wishes, and watch me float freely with the Sylphs of the air as I work in-conjunction with the faeries to magickly manifest your wishes into fruition.

DANDELION ~ WISHES

When you wish upon a star
My seeds of dreams will take them far
Upon the air now blow a gust
And focus on belief and trust
This magick is worked, with harm to none.
So mote it be. There, it is done.

28 **Monday**

29 Tuesday

Granny Boswell (1817–1909), well-known local witch in Cornwall.
Married The King of the Witches.

30 Wednesday

31 Thursday

1 Friday

New Moon · Second Witchcraft Act in England in 1562. Instigator was Elizabeth I.

2 Saturday

3 Sunday

4   Monday

5   Tuesday

6   Wednesday

7   Thursday

Anne Pedersdotter, Norwegian witch burnt to death in 1590.

8   Friday

FAERY MESSAGE

Don't be caught up in illusion for looks can be deceiving. Curiosity reveals only what you may wish to see, and confusion has hindered you from seeing that which is true. Glamour is my magick, of which my kind use to disguise themselves, make mischief or to move objects, just to distract you. My shining beauty will pull you in as I work with enchantments and place upon you charms, whilst crossing the realms of both Fae and Mortal. Waking daydreams of returning 'home' bridges the gap between our worlds, and deep communion with nature draws to you the ability to see the spirits of the wilds, and to access magickal connection through imagination. As I share with you dark faery secrets and natural alluring beauty tips, allow me to rub upon your eyes an ancient ointment to reveal all manner of disguise, for everything is not what it seems when it comes to working with the glamour of faery magick.

FAERY ~ GLAMOUR

Alluring spells, appeasing charm
'tis but beguilement to cause harm
Magick ointment rubbed on eyes
unveils illusion, reveals guise

---

9   Saturday
First Quarter Moon.

---

10   Sunday

WITCHY TIP

Work with the illusion of Glamour Magick to conceal ugliness or old age, in the guise of youthfulness and beauty. Shapeshift into animals and insects, such as butterflies, to glean secrets from unsuspecting others. Work an ancient faery charm to change eye or hair colour. Mirror reflection breaks the glamour.

---

11 Monday

---

12 Tuesday
Raven Grimassi (1951–2019), High Priest, Occultist, Wicca, Stregheria.

13   Wednesday
William Quan Judge (1851–1896), Occultist and Mystic, founder of the Theosophical Society.

14   Thursday

15   Friday
Channel Island Witch Trials (1550–1650), over 100 people accused, tortured and executed.

16   Saturday
Full Moon.

17   Sunday

18 Monday

19 Tuesday

20 Wednesday

21 Thursday

22 Friday

FLOWER FAERY INVOCATION

Hold the head of a flower of your choice in cupped hands.
As you gaze into it say:

I call on the Faeries, guardians of flowers.
Bestow upon me, your magickal powers.
I breathe in the fragrance, filling my heart.
Beauty surrounds me, ne'er to depart.
For all that is good, I ask with a kiss
Dear faeries of flowers, please grant me my wish.

Now breathe in the
fragrance deeply and say:

I work this Fae magick, with harm to none.
To heal and restore me, there it is done.

---

23 Saturday
Third Quarter Moon · Ursuline De Jesus was burned to death in 1754 in Brazil for witchcraft.

---

24 Sunday

BEAUTY SPELL

Sit in front of a mirror at dusk during a waxing crescent moon. Light a pink candle and start brushing your hair with a hairbrush as you say:

A magick mirror to look in and gaze
Flame lit glass reflects quite a haze
Peer within and then start to brush,
flowing locks slowly, do try to rush.
Focus upon the 'belle' within heart
Draw from its essence; a beautiful start
Image appears, see with new eyes
Perception reveals attractive surprise!

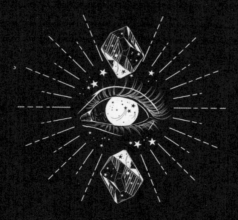

25 Monday

26 Tuesday

27 Wednesday

28 Thursday

29 Friday

30 Saturday
New Moon (Black Moon).

1   Sunday
Belthane · Third Witchcraft Act in England in 1604. Instigator was James I.

MAY

Hare, Milk, Bright and Willow Moon

A celebration of nature in full bloom.

The merry month of May is a celebration of when the energies of nature are at their strongest. For all of life is bursting with potent fertility, when the goddess is seeded by the god and we witness the conception of new life bursting forth into full bloom as the start of the Summer months to come.

BELTANE Northern Hemisphere: 1 May

GODDESS: Blodeuwedd (Celtic/Welsh), 'flower face', springtime flowers and new warmth

MAIDEN: In her fullness, sexuality, sensuality, passion, vitality and consummation

BELTANE

*The Maiden has reached her fullness
and is the manifestation of growth, sexuality, sensuality,
passion, vitality and consummation.*

This is the one age-old yearly Pagan celebration that continues to this day. Villagers gather to eat together and sup ale as they are treated to traditional Morris dancing and a May Queen is chosen. Local children weave ribbons in and out as they dance around a decorated maypole. This represents the traditional rituals that were once held to promote fertility for livestock and people alike.

Traditionally Beltane is a time of the blending of energies of the feminine and masculine, to celebrate the sacredness of sexuality. The goddess takes on the god as her lover, in order to give birth to the full bloom of nature during Summer months to come. Beltane marks the return of full life and nature is fully honoured in the fresh bright flowers, grasses and leaves that have started to push through. It is an abundant time of year when nature is at full bloom. Think maypoles – a phallic symbol to represent the potency of the God; May Queens, flower garlands and handfasting; Hawthorn, known as the 'May'; and the Lord and Lady of the Greenwood.

Beltane is celebrated as a Fire Festival to honour the Celtic Sun God, Bel. Great fires blazed from the hill tops as a sign of protection and others were lit for couples to leap over hand in hand before running into the woods to consummate their union. It is a time when goals, set at the beginning of the year come into fruition, when projects take off and relationships bloom. We sow our seeds at Imbolc and the goddess from her union with her consort gives birth to our goals, dreams and ideas, which spring into reality, and continue to grow and blossom into fruition.

BELTANE INCANTATION

With fires lit across the land,
A couple leaps whilst hand in hand,
To mark their union and this rite,
For they know tonight's the night!
As they run through darkened wood,
And find a grassy glade, they should,
Remember well of who's around,
For bands of faeries all surround,
The couple as they consummate,
The faeries cheer and seal the fate,
Of plants and flowers, shrubs and trees,
Whilst the god's upon his knees,
Impregnating the mother to be,
From sowing deep his natural seed.
And so in time the goddess will birth,
The magick that's nature, on this Earth.

2   Monday

3   Tuesday

---

4   Wednesday

---

5   Thursday

---

6   Friday

Margaret Read burned at the stake in Kings Lynn Norfolk in 1590.

---

7   Saturday

---

8   Sunday

9   Monday
First Quarter Moon.

10   Tuesday

11   Wednesday

12   Thursday

13   Friday
Ashkelon, Middle East in 1st century AD, 80 women executed for witchcraft.

14   Saturday

WITCH'S WISDOM

The energy of the cross quarter festival, Beltane, surrounds you now. This is the celebration of the God impregnating the Goddess, who in Mother form bursts forth the full growth of nature from Spring into the Summer months. Like the Goddess of Nature at this time, you too are nearly in full bloom. For the tiny seeds of creativity you planted earlier have developed and grown, their shoots have sprung and are ready to blossom. Time to cast aside all fears, which have darkened your outlook, and invite some warmth into your inner world if your sparkle has dimmed and your motivation has waned. What is it that truly makes your soul sing? An intense yearning is yet to be satisfied, although you are unsure of what it is you actually crave. Desire, attraction and enthusiasm accompany you as you remember and re-ignite that which fuels your passion. So spice up your life as you walk in your true light with full might, vitality and vigour to reclaim your zest for life. An ensured success will follow as you draw upon the gifts that the element of Fire offers, whose rites are honoured throughout the festival of Beltane, offering you the passion, desire, confidence and strength that accompanies you as you witness the birth of your dreams and goals, and fertility in all forms. As your ideas grow into fruition, taking action is key to bringing about desired results. Time to honour your sexuality and rites of woman/manhood. Time to celebrate.

INCANTATION

The God sows deep his natural seed.
Impregnates Goddess: Nature's need.
And from this union comes new birth.
Let's celebrate across the Earth.
This magick is worked, with harm to none
So mote it be. There, it is done.

15   Sunday

KITCHEN WITCHERY

CHOCOLATE – You've been starved of pleasure of late, and your desires to be desired are reaching boiling point. Let libido issues be a thing of the past as you seek pleasure from another source. Time to explore every sensual area until you are aroused by a lust for life and diverted from an unhealthy hedonistic lifestyle. For self-indulgence and a lack of restraint invites in addiction.

So I invite you to carefully peel back my wrapper and inhale the heady delights of my aroma. Allow your tastebuds to be tantalised as you become aroused by the erotic stimulant of my ingredients. I am the ultimate love potion. So pop me on your tongue and allow the power of Aphrodite, the Goddess of Love, to slide smoothly down your throat and deeply embrace the warm, stimulative effects of my love-philtre. So let's get in the mood as you light a few candles, play some soft music and indulge your senses to get your mojo back!

WITCHY RECIPE

Chocolate Face Mask – For an antioxidant spa treatment at home

Melt 2 bars of dark chocolate in a bowl. Mix in 2/3 cup of milk, 1 teaspoon of salt and 3 tablespoons of sugar. Allow it to cool and then apply to face and neck. Leave for 20 minutes and rinse off with lukewarm water. Almost instantly you will notice smooth and soft skin.

16   Monday
Full Moon.

17 Tuesday

18 Wednesday

Cassandra Latham Jones was the first person in the United Kingdom
who registered her work as a witch with the inland revenue in 1996.

19 Thursday

20 Friday

21 Saturday

22 Sunday

Third Quarter Moon.

23 Monday
Kenneth Grant (1924–2011), Ceremonial Magician and an advocate of the Thelemic religion.

24 Tuesday

25 Wednesday

26 Thursday

27 Friday

28 Saturday

CHOCOLATE ~ APHRODISIAC

Food of Love, Goddess Divine
Sensual pleasure's purely mine
Taste me to arouse desire
My delights will take you higher
This magick is worked, with harm to none.
So mote it be. There, it is done.

PASSION SPELL

Face the direction of South at noon.
Light a red candle and say:

I call upon the spirit of Fire,
invoking vigour, adoration, desire.
Allow the fire to ravage and surge
to re-ignite my hot-blooded urge.
Apathy fades in soft candlelight
Stoke up the flame of passion tonight
Emotions embraced and ready to heal
Passion aroused now, with fervour and zeal.

Snuff the candle flame out and direct the smoke from
the extinguished flame over your heart centre.

29   Sunday

JUNE

Moon of Horses, Hawthorn, Strawberry Moon

Glorifying the full strength and light of the Sun.

June is busting out all over as we celebrate the full bloom of roses, honeysuckle and warmer weather. Named after the Roman goddess Juno, the goddess of marriage, sunny June sees the start of the wedding season, and a June bride is considered to be lucky. June is also the halfway stage of the growing season for farmers, a traditional midpoint between planting and harvesting. The Goddess is now the Mother, and the Sun God is at the height of his virility and life-giving power. Celebrations of fullness, expansiveness and achievements are awash with joy as the light reaches its peak and we enjoy the longest day and shortest night of the Wheel of the Year.

LITHA Northern Hemisphere: 21 June

GODDESS: Aine (Celtic/Irish), faery queen of Summer, growth, love, luck and magick

MOTHER: In her full power and strength.

LITHA

*Empowerment, celebration of light
and full strength of the Sun.*

This is the month that celebrates the Sun festival known as Litha, or Summer Solstice, which is when the sun is at its highest point in the sky, and at its strongest. It is a time of intensification, of focus, development and determination as we connect with the sun to become stronger and to claim our full self-power in celebration, honour and ritual. Those who are not aware of such connotation still, albeit unwittingly, worship the sun in other ways. For they partake in outdoor parties, barbecues and top up their tans during hot and sunny days. Celtic tradition, honoured through tales and legends, tells of a great battle that plays out at this time of year between the mighty Holly King and the majestic Oak King. At Summer Solstice the Holly King wins supreme and stands proud through to Winter, until at Yule he is cut down in his prime when Oak King wins and presides over the coming months through until their next battle at Litha.

This is a time of year when we can tap into Midsummer magick, for the veil between worlds is thin. Think Titania, Oberon, faery spells and faery rings of mushrooms, toadstools and flowers where those with an open heart are invited in, to connect with the natural magick of the Fae.

MIDSUMMER INVOCATION

As I enter within this magickal ring,
My heart is open and ready to sing,
Songs of the wood, words of the Fae,
Who guide me in, and show me the way.
I call on the magick of Midsummer's Eve,
Whose mystic and mystery together doth weave.
May power bestow me this very night,
As I share my found gifts, for t'is only right.
With arms outstretched to the magickal ones,
I give honour and thanks, and so now it's done.

30 Monday

New Moon · Joan of Arc (1412-1431), visionary. Burnt for heresy and witchcraft.

31 Tuesday

---

1 Wednesday

Fourth Witchcraft Act in England in 1735. The law abolished hunting
and executions of witches in the United Kingdom.

---

2 Thursday

New Moon.

---

3 Friday

---

4 Saturday

---

5 Sunday

WITCH'S WISDOM

The intensification of the full sun at Litha shines upon you as you step up to the next level in all that you do. This is a time of focus, development and determination as you become stronger and claim the full self-power you are aiming towards. Dare to explore every avenue open to you and do the unexpected. A new gateway has opened and you may find that you leave others behind, as your unwavering dedication leads you away. Fear not, for the light of the sun will highlight the path of unfamiliar territory and borrow, if you will, the sun's strength and warmth as you embrace these times of study, focus and concentration. Diversions may come to tempt you along the way. You may be blind for a while as you stumble upon the unknown, but nevertheless try to remember that these are merely tests of your commitment. Intensifying commitment will increase your self-power. What you have been waiting for comes into fruition during the Summer months. Time to shine brightly, so don't give away your personal power. Instead move forward fearlessly and call upon the strength of the Sun God to break through.

The Sun Gods shine favourably on you and remind you that the answer to prayer, and the outcome of spells, happen in mysterious ways. Time to trust the Mystery.

INCANTATION

In all that I do, and all that is done,
Bringer of life and Midsummer Sun,
Intensifies and gifts me strength,
To claim my power, at any length.
This magick is worked, with harm to. none
So mote it be. There, it is done

6   Monday

Alex Sanders (1926-1988), Occultist and High Priest, founder of Alexandrian Wicca.

7   Tuesday
First Quarter Moon · Swein Macdonald (1931–2003), Highland Seer, Mystic and Occultist.

8   Wednesday

9   Thursday

10   Friday
First hangings of witche s at Gallows Hill, Salem, United States. Bridget Bishop was the first witch hanged in 1692.

11   Saturday

12   Sunday

13   Monday
Gerald Gardner (1884–1964), High Priest, Founder of Gardnerian Wicca.

14   Tuesday
Full Moon

15   Wednesday
Muree bin Ali-al Asiri was beheaded for witchcraft in Saudi Arabia in 2012.

16   Thursday

17   Friday

WITCHY TIP

Working with fire energy, in an etheric sense, is a great healing. Imagining etheric flames purging through any negative energy, raging and consuming any darkness that lies within oneself, which has formed from any negative thoughts and feelings, helps to move one forward and gets rid of what no longer serves.

18 Saturday

19 Sunday

JUNE

20 Monday

21 Tuesday

Litha (Summer Solstice) · Third Quarter Moon.

22 Wednesday

23 Thursday

24 Friday

EMPOWERMENT SPELL

At the magickal time of noon, light a red
candle and gaze into the flame. With arms
stretched up towards the Sun, say:

I call down the Sun, spirit of Fire
Bring me your courage and all I desire
Extinguish the dark that blacks out the light
So I am released of my fears and all plight
Allow the fire to ravage through me
Empowerment stoked, setting me free
Inner flame's re-ignited to grow
For now I become the sacred glow.

When you feel that this is completed blow
out the candle. Let the swirl of the extinguished
flame wrap around you and say:

Gratefully I accept the power of you
Of strength to assist in all that I do
Shine through me brightly, build magick in me
Assist my transcendence, so mote it be.

---

25 Saturday

---

26 Sunday

27 Monday
Scott Cunningham (1956–1993). Author on Wicca and Herbalism.

28 Tuesday

29 Wednesday
New Moon.

30 Thursday

1 Friday
Witchcraft Act in England repealed in 1951 and replaced with the Fraudulent Mediums Act.

KITCHEN WITCHERY

CINNAMON – If your spirit has been dampened and your light has dimmed, if what once brought you joy has waned as you face the challenges and responsibilities life has dealt you, allow the sun of Litha to shine upon you. For what once aroused you and your motivation has been diluted as a veil of cynicism cloaks your connection to the magickal realms. It's time to see through new eyes with wonder and awe to discover a world you've long forgotten. My high vibration will assist in increasing your frequency to reach a higher state of spirituality. So add fuel to the fire by inviting me to trigger the passion within you, for new zeal is what's required. As the flames lick away old hurts and wounds they are replaced by a sacred glow which re-ignites a spark of desire, focus and intent. Just a pinch of me, in powder form, will supercharge your energy and power level to stimulate your true essence and rekindle the magick in your life.

CINNAMON ~ RE-IGNITE

Power's gone, faded light
Spark within needs to ignite
Eat a freshly baked warm roll
To boost your body, spirit, soul.
This magick is worked, with harm to none.
So mote it be. There, it is done.

---

2   Saturday

---

3   Sunday

JULY

Hay, Thunder, Mead, Oak Moon

The power of Summer burns brightly,
intensifying passion and destiny.

The month of July signifies the height of Summer in all its glorious radiance, in the Northern Hemisphere, as the sun beats down upon the optimum abundance of nature's full bloom. Now's the time to enjoy the gifts of the Mother Goddess, for your work is done.

The magick of Summer invites intense energies of lust, passion, attraction, illumination, love, sex, sun and heat. So put down your tools, have fun and enjoy the carefree days of Summer. Taking a well-deserved break to rejuvenate and have some fun is essential for your well-being on all levels. Be careful not to get burned as you enjoy outdoor parties, barbecues and sunbathing during this hot, passionate month, as you worship the sun and harness the power of the element of fire. In magickal terms, the intensity of high noon is a perfect time to cast spells as you face the direction of South. As the heat of the sun breathes renewed passion into your workings, as well as relationships, you attract the energy of abundance, awakening your spiritual kundalini energy through lust, attraction and desire, as you draw down the sun.

As the sun greets you it highlights the path you are to take towards your destiny, in order for you to complete your life's mission.

GODDESS: Etain (Celtic/Irish), The Shining One,
Sun and Moon goddess, lights the way on the path of
transformation, towards balance, wholeness and rebirth.

MOTHER: Uncovering the light and strength
within, beauty, sun, love, vitality of life.

SUMMER INCANTATION

Ignite the passion of Summer, and know,
You are the power, the sacred glow.
Love and passion stirred and invoked.
Abundance is yours now the fire is stoked.
Lounging, bronzing in the sun.
Sea salt air and having fun.
Food delights, cocktails too.
Take this well-earned break, for you
To be restored, take the charge.
Enjoy the rest now. Bon Voyage!

4   Monday

5   Tuesday
Lucy Cavendish (1961), best-selling author, Witch, Druid.

6   Wednesday

7   Thursday
First Quarter Moon..

8   Friday

9   Saturday

10   Sunday

KITCHEN WITCHERY

ALOE VERA - I have come to soothe you, to bring new peace and alleviate your discomfort. So allow me to heal and reduce your pain through my natural anti-inflammatory effects. I am known as the 'plant of immortality' and invite you to cut my spiky but succulent leaf and peel away the hard skin to find inside a soothing gel, effective enough to calm any irritation or inflammation. I am a powerful antioxidant who offers unique therapeutic properties, especially when applied as an ointment for your skin and gums, and when used in a beauty regime. I shall thrive if you pop me in a clay pot on your sunniest windowsill, to be on hand as a soothing magickal amulet against accidents and misfortunes, especially around the home.

ALOE VERA ~ SOOTHE

Soothing gel to heal the skin.
Digestive tract heals from within.
Inflammation, immune disease,
my golden juice will bring you ease.
This magick is worked, with harm to none.
So mote it be. There, it is done.

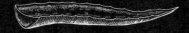

11   Monday

12 Tuesday

13 Wednesday

Full Moon · Margaret Murray (1863–1963), Egyptologist, archaeologist, Occultist and Folklorist. The first woman to be appointed as a lecturer in a uniarsity in 1898. · John Dee (1527–1608), Court astronomer to Elizabeth I of England, Occultist, Alchemist and Mystic.

14 Thursday

15 Friday

16 Saturday

17 Sunday

Chelmsford Assizes (which was the periodic court for serious crime and witch trials), Essex, England. Elizabeth Francis (1529–1579) convicted three times for bewitchment and witchcraft. She was executed after the third trial.

JULY

---

18 Monday

---

19 Tuesday

Second hangings of Salem witches in the United States. Five women convicted in 1692.

---

20 Wednesday

Third Quarter Moon.

---

21 Thursday

---

22 Friday

Mother Agnes Waterhouse (1503–1566), first woman executed in England for witchcraft.

WITCHY RECIPE

Aloe Vera Gel – Used to treat serve burns,
sunburn, small cuts, dry skin.

With a sharp knife, slice off an outer leaf of the plant.
Drain out the gel/sap by placing the leaves upright in a cup.
Scoop out the gel from the cup with a spoon into a
clean sterilised glass jar. Keep in the fridge. You can also
freeze the gel into an ice cube tray to use as needed.

WITCHY TIP

DAISY – Holds the energy of the sun within its
yellow centre, and that of the moon within its
white petals. The petals open up to follow the
circle of sun all through the day, folding its
petals around the yellow middle when the
sun goes down and the moon ascends.
Ingesting a daisy is completely safe and
connects one to the frequency of both
sun and moon, thus the balancing of
male and female energies within.

23 Saturday

24 Sunday

DESTINY SPELL

Light a red candle and face the direction of South.
Raise your arms up towards the Full Moon and say:

Call down the moon to reflect the sun
Invoking a life spell that can't be undone
A path that glitters to be revealed
Focus and follow, for fate has been sealed
Destiny's signposts now point the way
Life purpose embraced, go seize it today!
This magick is worked, with harm to none.
So mote it be. There, it is done.

Blow out the candle and direct the extinguished
flame to smoke over your solar plexus chakra
for ultimate confidence.

25   **Monday**

26 Tuesday

27 Wednesday

York Assizes (which was the periodic court for serious crime and witch trials). Pendle witch trials started in 1612.

28 Thursday

New Moon · Huntington Assizes (which was the periodic court for serious crime and witch trials). Mary Hickes, Witch of Huntington and her nine-year-old daughter both hanged for witchcraft in 1716.

29 Friday

Jennet Preston, hanged at York Racecourse in 1612. · Sarah Good hanged with four other women from the Salem witch trials, United States, 1612.

30 Saturday

31 Sunday

AUGUST
Corn, Holly and Grain Moon

Celebration and gratitude of the grain harvest

This heady month of sun and fun is greeted as a time of opportunity and good fortune. For these are the care-free days of Summer, when the dreams that were seeded at Imbolc come fully into fruition and are now ripe for the picking. We witness the first hint of Autumn as the hottest part of Summer makes its promise to wane, through its shortened days and the first grains ready to be harvested. It's time to reap the harvest of rewards and to appreciate and bless everything that comes your way, as we make the most of the remaining light and warm weather before the Fall, and give thanks for the abundance of the growth of the passing season.

LUGHNASADH / LAMMAS
Northern Hemisphere: 1 August

GODDESS: Tailtiu (Celtic/Irish), Goddess of August, of the earth, the harvest and first grains. She is the foster mother of the Sun God, Lugh.

MOTHER: Matures, gratitude for earthly, physical sustenance

LUGHNASADH / LAMMAS

Gratitude for gifts of the earth.

Lughnasadh, or Lammas, marks the very first harvest of the year and the gathering in of the grains. It is when the Sun God Lugh is celebrated, aka John Barleycorn who is cut down in his prime, only to rise up again the following year. This is an important and busy time of year that our ancestors looked forward to. A time of plenty, for feasting in celebration of the first harvest and for honouring the natural cycle of life, death and rebirth, represented as the spirit of John Barleycorn, also known as Jack-in-the-Green and Robin Hood! His time will come again. But for now, the seeds planted earlier in the year have grown into an abundant crop and are ready to be harvested and stored in the grain barns, to see out the cold and barren months to come.

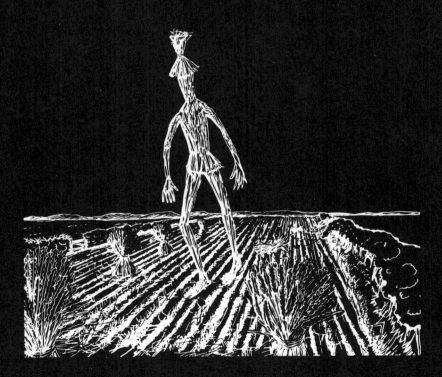

LUGHNASADH INVOCATION

Today the wheel of the year doth stop,
At Lammas, time to reap the crops,
that were sown earlier this year.
Celebrate the harvest cheer,
Of wheat, of cereal, of the grain.
Store it safely, before the wane.
John Barleycorn is now cut down,
From his prime, but look around.
For Lugh the Sun God shines from high,
Over the fields from the sky.
From Mother Earth we are blessed,
Toil now over, soon can rest.
But from the sow, what did you reap?
Is it good, or do you weep?
From hard work what have you earned?
Of the lesson, what is learnt?
May the magick of this day,
Bless you now, in every way.

1   Monday

Lughnasadh · Fraudulent Mediums Act of 1951 replaced in 2008.

2   Tuesday

3   Wednesday

4   Thursday

5   Friday

First Quarter Moon · Malin Matsdotter (1613–1676), originally from Sweden and of Finnish descent and was burnt as a witch.

6   Saturday

7   Sunday

WITCH'S WISDOM

Lughnasadh brings great tidings of prosperity to you. Your planted seeds have grown into an abundant crop and now the harvest has been reaped. A time of opportunity and good fortune is upon you. Like the care-free days of Summer, everything is going your way. The venture, in whatever form, you put your heart and soul into is ready to flourish. Your dreams have been answered and your spells for good fortune are ripe for the picking. Success is yours and like a true alchemist, everything you touch right now turns to gold. So don't let a single opportunity pass you by. For you are supported as you walk your rightful path, as your positive attitude and gratitude leads to good fortune. This is what you've been waiting to hear. So enjoy every moment and remember to appreciate and bless everything that comes your way. Your days of famine are no more, it's time to reap the rewards and feast upon the good you have created, as the Sun God Lugh shines upon you.

INCANTATION

Abundant days are here at last.
Time to feast, no need to fast.
Celebrate! Sing, dance and leap.
Harvest's in. T'is mine to reap.
This magick is worked, with harm to none.
So mote it be. There, it is done.

9 Tuesday

Akua Dentch in Ghana was beaten to death for witchcraft in 2020.

10 Wednesday

Witches World Day established against witch hunts created after Akua Dentch was killed in Ghana on 9 August.

11 Thursday

12 Friday

Full Moon · Madame Helen Blavatsky (1831–1891), Russian Occultist, Philosopher. Co-founder of the Theosophical society.

13 Saturday

14 Sunday

15   Monday

___

16   Tuesday

___

17   Wednesday

___

18   Thursday

Lancaster Assizes (which was the periodic court for serious crime and witch trials) held in 1612.
Pendle and Samlesbury witches, 9 women and 1 man found guilty of witchcraft.

___

19   Friday

Third Quarter Moon · Salem witch trials held in the United States in 1692, 1 woman and five
men hanged for witchcraft.

WITCHY RECIPE

Bay Leaf Shampoo – For silky hair, dandruff, itchy scalp, gets rid of lice

Take one cup of spring water, place in a saucepan and bring to the boil. Add the dried bay leaves, reduce the heat and simmer for a couple of minutes. Strain the mixture, remove the bay leaves and set aside to cool. Once cooled, add 1/3 of a cup each of Castile soap, jojoba oil and approximately 20 to 26 drops of essential oil of your choice. Pour into a clean storage bottle.
Shake before you use it.

20 Saturday
Pendle witches hung at Gallows Hill in Lancaster, United Kingdom in 1612.

21 Sunday

BAY LEAVES ~ ABUNDANCE

Don't give up, or give in
Being rich is not a sin
Accept all gifts that come your way
Abundance is yours now to stay
This magick is worked, with harm to none.
So mote it be. There, it is done.

ABUNDANCE SPELL

Drop a coin in a jar at dawn during
a New Moon phase, and say:

Jar of abundance, vessel of wealth
I focus on healing my financial health
Placed in the wealth corner of room
A coin dropped each day breaks miserly gloom
I'll relax so that money flows in easily
And all that I wish for, to come unto me
Yellow Citrine invites fortune in
So too doth green, I'll wear it to win!

Leave your money jar in the wealth corner (southeast)
of a room to invite in and maintain magickal prosperity.

22 Monday

23 Tuesday

24 Wednesday

25 Thursday

26 Friday

27 Saturday
New Moon.

28 Sunday

AUGUST

29 Monday

30 Tuesday

31 Wednesday

Raymond Buckland (1934-2017), High Priest and Occultist.

1 Thursday

First law passed on spells and witchcraft in The Code of Hammurabi from 1754BC in Ancient Mesopotamia.

2 Friday

KITCHEN WITCHERY

BAY LEAVES – It's been a struggle and you've been going without unnecessarily for too long now. Your cries for prosperity have been heard, so please don't give up on all that you have worked so hard for already. Don't you realise that everything you need to support you on your magickal path is ready to be supplied? All you need do is accept that an abundance of prosperity is your birth-right, and to work a little magick! My magickal properties will assist you against misfortune, and a dried leaf, with your desires written on it, will bring your wishes into fruition, if burnt. Pop one of my leaves in your purse or wallet and soon your inner storeroom will be overflowing with a plenitude of riches. Lughnasadh marks a time of opulence and soon you will forget the miserable empty days of late. So remember to count the cornucopia of blessings you receive and rejoice in any serendipitous moments, for they are signs of the new and lucrative phase you've been waiting for.

3   Saturday
First Quarter Moon.

4   Sunday

SEPTEMBER

Harvest, Hazel, Fruit and Barley Moon

A time for gathering, resting, reflecting and celebration.

As the cycle of the natural world moves further towards completion of the Wheel of the Year, we find ourselves on the cusp of transition, just before the year begins to wane into darkness.

Following the celebration of the grain harvest at Lughnasadh, which is now fully in and stored, we acknowledge the abundance and ripeness of the fruits of the earth, which the Harvest Queen bestows upon us at this time of year. The goddess is found in her Mother aspect in the fading Summer twilight or in the harvest moon. As the full life of Summer comes to an end we become witness to ripe fruits, nuts, squashes and the flaming colours of red, orange and gold of Autumn as nature turns in on herself, with the promise of darker barren months of Winter to come. This was a time of preparation, gathering and storing for our ancestors, as the final harvest of fruits and vegetables was brought in to last through the Winter months. Traditionally workers were paid for the upcoming year, annual dues were collected and accounts were balanced. Nature's gifts are in abundance and as the soft autumnal sun declines and autumnal mists descend, soft, ripe fruit falls gently from heavily laden trees. Time to celebrate and draw from earth's bounty.

MABON Northern Hemisphere: 21 September

GODDESS: Banbha (Celtic/Irish), earth mother, protection, fruitfulness, keeper of mystery

MOTHER: Contemplation, self-sufficiency and balance

MABON

*When day and night is in balance
and the fruit harvest is celebrated.*

Mabon is a recent name, but has been adopted by witches and pagans alike to celebrate the Autumn Equinox, when daylight and darkness are in balance with each other, night and day are of equal length and in perfect equilibrium – dark and light, masculine and feminine, inner and outer. The name Mabon is associated with the Welsh god of Mythology, Mabon, and also with Faery Queen Mab who rules over the Unseelie Court of Autumn and Winter.

At this time of balance and celebration we are reminded that we too are a part of nature. This is the time of going deep within, to rest after the labour of harvest, for reflection, to count our blessings and for the abundance that has been bestowed upon us throughout the year, thus far. We must look at where we have been, and what has been done during the preceding months and to give thanks, which in turn will truly fill both our inner and outer gifts. For this is when you reap what you had sown earlier in the year, and to harvest all that's now been made manifest, from your earlier dreams and aspirations. Likewise it's a good time to let go of all that is no longer necessary and watch them fall away, just as the leaves do, at this time of year. As you acknowledge and embrace your shadow side bring it into balance with the light that you already exude. Draw from the power of the cornucopia of abundance, a symbol for the wealth of harvest at Mabon and balance your masculine and feminine energies, in order to be both giving and receptive at this time of year in gratitude and perfect equilibrium.

MABON INCANTATION

Autumn's upon us, here at last.
A time to reflect upon the past,
Of the year that seems to have flown.
Dreams were planted, now have grown.
Mabon gifts us dark and light
Of perfect balance both day and night
And so we look deep down within
To check our equilibrium
Look back on past hurts, lessons learned.
And use them so you won't get burnt.
Important to shine out far and wide
And to honour shadow side
For both together makes you whole,
The two as one completes your soul.
Light two candles, one black, one white.
Representing your joy and plight.
Eliminate all you do not need
But keep what you have to succeed
The harvest's in, we give great cheer,
And thanks for an abundant year.

5   Monday

6 Tuesday

7 Wednesday

Margaret Inne Quaine and John Cubbon, executed in Castletown, Isle of Man in 1617. There is a memory plaque on Smelt Monument.

8 Thursday

9 Friday

10 Saturday

Full Moon · Tiberius Claudius executed 45 men and 85 woman in 345 AD for witchcraft.

11 Sunday

Silver Raven Wolf (1956-), author of *Witchcraft and Wicca*.

WITCH'S WISDOM

Mabon gifts you with the balance of light and dark. At this fruitful time you are reminded that you too are a part of nature. Therefore it is harvest time for you too. What seeds did you plant in your life this year? Have they come to fruition? What do you need to bring in, or release, in order to move forward? Mabon asks you to reach into your very own storehouse to seek the balance within. If you're feeling restlessness, emotional or out of sorts then call upon Mabon to restore the balance in your life. Work with all elements in ritual and magick in equal measure, and honour each equally on your altar for a time until you find a healthy balance in all things. Embrace any aspect of you which is devoid of light, and eliminate only that which does not serve you, with gratitude and lessons learned. Reflect upon the past, holding onto only the lessons. Look at what is causing an imbalance in your life. Eliminate anything/anyone who upsets the equilibrium. Embrace and get to fully know your shadow side.

Once balance is achieved, rest and enjoy the fruits of your personal harvest.

MABON INCANTATION

Mabon gifts us dark and light
Light two candles; one black, one white.
Important to shine out far and wide,
And to honour shadow side.
This magick is worked, with harm to none.
So mote it be. There, it is done.

12   Monday

13 Tuesday

14 Wednesday

15 Thursday

16 Friday

17 Saturday
Third Quarter Moon.

18 Sunday

19 Monday
Fulda witch trials in Germany between 1603–1606. Merga Bien (1560–1603) burned alive.

20 Tuesday

21 Wednesday
Mabon (Autumn Equinox).

22 Thursday
Salem witch trials in the United States between 1692–1693, 8 people hanged for witchcraft.

23 Friday

24 Saturday
North Berwick witch trials in United Kingdom between 1590–1592, 70 people executed.

KITCHEN WITCHERY

APPLE – I am the forbidden fruit. Not because I am bad for you, but because I unveil that which is hidden. When you slice me in half, my five seeds reveal a star, the Pentagram, the exact same shape that Venus, the planet of love, forms when orbiting the earth. I invite you to bite through my ripe skin to taste my sweet flesh for I am the fruit of the harvest who holds the secret knowledge that all witches seek.

WITCH'S RECIPE

Apple Cider Vinegar – Used for lowering blood
sugar and cholesterol.

Using a clean jar, fill the jar three-quarters full of either chopped organic apples or apple scrap. Dissolve 1 tablespoon of cane sugar into a cup of water and pour over apples until they are covered. Weight the apples down under the water with a small glass jar. Cover with cheesecloth and secure with a rubber band. Store in a dark room for approximately 3 weeks. Strain the apples pieces out and return the liquid to the jar. Put back in dark room for another 3 to 4 weeks stirring every couple of days. Keep tasting until it's right for you.

25 Sunday
New Moon.

APPLE ~ HIDDEN

*Don't ignore what is forbidden
One bite reveals all that's hidden
Pentagram of seeds revealed
Five pointed star now claimed and sealed
This magick is worked, with harm to none.
So mote it be. There, it is done.*

BALANCE SPELL

Hold a red jasper crystal in each hand and place a piece
of High John Root at your feet during a Dark Moon.
Hold your arms out to the side and say:

*Scales of Justice to weigh up all blight
Release judgements keeps my heart light
Growing the root of High John, in my mind
Removes all obstacles. Like-wise in kind,
fairness, justness, objectivity,
integral behaviour now sets me free.
Shadows and light, authentic and true
Balance achieved to start anew.*

Visualise the High John Root removing any obstacles in your way
as you imagine it growing within. Hold the red jasper on each hand
until you feel in perfect balance. So mote it be.

26   Monday

27 Tuesday

28 Wednesday

29 Thursday

30 Friday

1 Saturday
It is estimated that over 200,000 witches were burnt or hung in Western Europe.

2 Sunday
Arthur Edward Waite (1857-1942), Occultist, Magician, Alchemist and co-creator of the Rider-Waite tarot.

OCTOBER

Blood, Vine and Hunters Moon

Season of witches, the old year dies.

October is the month where we witness the death of nature. As leaves continue to fall in the Northern Hemisphere we enjoy the vibrant colours of the season, an abundance of squashes and darker nights. Now that the harvest is in and celebrated at Mabon, it's a time to prepare fruit jam preserves and tinctures for colds and flu, using ingredients collected from the earth, trees and hedgerows earlier, such as rose hips, apples and berries. The Crone, who reigns over the harsher months, is cold, callous and now beckons you with a bony finger, to witness the death of nature and all that will assist you moving forward.

SAMHAIN Northern Hemisphere: 31 October

GODDESS: Cerridwen (Celtic/Welsh), keeper of the gates between the worlds, grail goddess

CRONE: Bringer of darkness and death, of blood and bone, the underworld

SAMHAIN

*An honouring of the souls of the dead, when
the veil between the worlds are thinnest.*

Hallowe'en conjures up ghosts, pumpkin lanterns and children shouting, 'Trick or Treat!' as they hungrily hold out bags for candy and celebrated at the end of October in both hemispheres. However, traditionally called Samhain, this is an old Celtic celebration of Summer's End. Fires were lit on the night of 31 October in the Northern Hemisphere, and villagers would burn crops and animals to their gods and goddesses to share with them and to give thanks for the bounty of the harvest. The Celts believed that the souls of the dead of the Underworld were set free for that night, of which some were welcomed and others feared. Costumes and masks were worn were for protection from these spirits.

The veil between the worlds at this time is at its thinnest where we are more able to see and connect with the world of Faery and Spirit.

Samhain is still considered a time of connection and reflection on those who have left this world for the other, and to look at where we ourselves have journeyed from and to, during the wheel of the year. The Goddess, in her triple form, has become the Crone and we are invited to draw on her wisdom from deep within, as she cradles us during the dark months to come, enabling us to release all that no longer serves us.

3 Monday
First Quarter Moon.

---

4 Tuesday

---

5 Wednesday

---

6 Thursday

---

7 Friday

---

8 Saturday

SAMHAIN INCANTATION

Cauldrons boiling, lanterns are shining.
Ghouls and ghosts, groans and whining.
Parties sweep across the land.
Children, adults, hand in hand.
Time of fun but must remember,
As fires burn bright and glow with embers,
Our ancestors who walked before.
We honour thee and ask for more,
Wisdom, tools, to help us be,
The wise amongst us, let us see,
Through veil, whilst thin, this very night.
Protection in place, no need for fright.
So we welcome you and all you bring.
Go deep inside and look within,
To shed the old, a shamanic death,
Embraced and warmed within the earth.
Inviting in life anew.
The goddess calls for it to be you.
Through the year from maiden to mother,
The end is now, to feel the other.
In her glory stands the Crone.
Don't be afraid to stand alone.
This sacred path leads you to be free.
Go forth in strength, so mote it be.

---

9   Sunday

Full Moon · Flavia Kate Peters (1968–), High Priestess, Faery Seer, Occultist, United Kingdom.

WITCH'S WISDOM

Death appears before you now in the form of Samhain. Time to let go, to surrender and accept that death is never final. It is simply a portal to re-birthing into the next and glorious stage of the cycle called life. This is a time of connection and reflection on those who have left this world for the other, and to look at where you have journeyed from and to, during the wheel of the year. The goddess, in her triple form, has become the Crone and you are invited to draw on her wisdom from deep within, as she cradles you during the dark months to come. She will protect and guide you through this period of the dark night of the soul, and you will emerge wiser and more powerful than you could ever imagine.

INCANTATION

Through veil, whilst thin, this very night.
Protection placed, no need for fright.
Crone welcomes you and all you bring.
Wisdom waits, now look within.
This magick is worked, with harm to none.
So mote it be. There, it is done.

_____

11   Tuesday

_____

12   Wednesday
Aleister Crowley (1875–1947), English Occultist, High Priest, Ceremonial Magician.

_____

13   Thursday
All Templars living in France in 1307 were arrested and condemned for witchcraft and heresy. This is the origin of Friday the thirteenth being unlucky.

_____

14   Friday
Patricia Crowther (1927–), early mother of modern Wicca, High Priestess.

_____

15   Saturday

_____

16   Sunday

ANCESTORS

Remembering those who have walked before you, and understanding their ways will help to you to release any hurts and pains. Healing ancestral lines will enable you to break free and step into the freedom your soul yearns for, to be whole and complete. Remembrance asks you to honour the ancestors, for those who lived their lives trusting in, recognising and interacting with the spirits of the land and living in accordance with the magickal law of nature. Call upon their wisdom to assist you in awakening to the magick of the old ways, of the days when nature was respected and the natural balance in all things was ensured. Remember too who you are and where you have come from, and honour yourself for never giving up, as you walk in the footsteps of the ancestors.

INCANTATION

Ancestors of blood and bone.
From Earth you have to Spirit, flown.
Ancestral lines now heal at last,
And break free from the chains of past.
This magick is worked, with harm to none
So mote it be. There, it is done.

17 Monday
Third Quarter Moon.

18 Tuesday

19 Wednesday

20 Thursday

Selena Fox (1949–), Wiccan Priestess and Pagan Elder.

21 Friday

22 Saturday

Witch trials of 1674–1675 held in Torsaker, Sweden, 71 beheaded and burnt as witches.

23 Sunday

24 Monday

Over 2000 magickal books burnt by Emperor Augustus of Rome in 31 BC.

25 Tuesday

New Moon.

26 Wednesday

27 Thursday

28 Friday

29 Saturday

KITCHEN WITCHERY

BLACK PEPPER – When your world becomes negatively affected by someone or something else it is time for a little banishment magick! Call on the strength of black pepper to assist in performing any kind of banishment ritual, to flush out all forms of lower emotions that have been directed your way, such as jealousy, anger and resentment. Burn black pepper in your home or carry some black pepper seeds in your pocket as a charm to ward off any hurt that has been intended for you, and you shall be liberated to freely work your magick, with harm to none. So mote it be.

WITCH'S RECIPE

BLACK PEPPER INCENSE – Used for protection, banishing, nightmares.

Take a pinch of black pepper and charcoal from a fire and grind together using a mortar and pestle. Add a pinch of sea salt. Make sure the mixture stays black and does not turn to grey. Once mixed, transfer into a fireproof vessel and using the mixture as a base add a cone of incense on top. When the cone has burned out, mix the two together. Store in an airtight container or glass bottle.

BLACK PEPPER ~ BANISHMENT

Beware! Be warned! Be free from harm
Use peppercorns as magick charm
Spite of tongue or curs-ed deeds
I'll banish with my pepper seeds
This magick is worked, with harm to none.
So mote it be. There, it is done.

---

30 Sunday

PROTECTION SPELL

Stand under a New Moon at midnight. Sprinkle a circle of salt around you. Hold a lit black candle in one hand as you face North and in the other hand hold a grounding piece of Black Tourmaline crystal and say:

Star of protection, a circle of salt
Surround and safeguard me from any default
Guard me from danger, gossip and hurt,
from those who may curse me and dish out the dirt.
I call upon the elements, five,
preserve my intentions, so I can survive.
Standing within, I lift up my arms
Black candle and crystal now banishes harm
Keep safe and defend my energy flow,
as I raise my vibration, allow me to grow.
Now out of danger protection in place
Magickal work now safe to embrace.

SALT

Allow me to absorb the psychic energy that you have unwittingly received by sprinkling me around you in a circle, across the thresholds or perimeters of your dwelling, or wear me in a pocket or pouch. I will defend your honour and ensure that you are shielded as your sensitivity increases. Protection is key as you open yourself up to a higher spiritual vibration, so call on me to safeguard you as you work your magick.

---

31   Monday

Samhain (Hallowe'en).

1   Tuesday

First Quarter Moon · In 331 BC over 170 women were executed in Rome for witchcraft.

2   Wednesday

3   Thursday

Petronilla De Meath was burnt at the stake in Kilkenny Ireland in 1324. This was the first known case in Ireland and the United Kingdom of death by fire for heresy.

4   Friday

5   Saturday

6   Sunday

Mother Shipton (1488–1561), Prophetess, Soothsayer and Witch.

NOVEMBER

Snow, Ivy, Dark Moon

Re-assessment, embracing loss and acceptance

Happy New Year! After the death of the year that we witnessed at Samhain, 1 November is celebrated by witches as All Hallow's Day, the start of the new Celtic year and the beginning of Winter. However, November is regarded as an autumnal month which offers a mix of cold and bright, as burnt-orange leaves continue to fall in the now rather chilly Northern Hemisphere. The weather can be confusing with its bright sunshine accompanying much colder days, which brings with it the promise of hard frost and sometimes snow. It is a good time to defend yourself and to define your boundaries with others during these harsh, biting days and for darker magick to ward off harm.

However, as we prepare to face the harshness of Winter yet to come, in the Northern Hemisphere, we can rejoice in a month of festivities of thanksgiving, fireworks and of remembrance. It is a time of rain and of great storms. A good time for Weather Witching!

GODDESS: The Morrighan (Irish/Celtic), Battle goddess of death and war, bane magick and darker arts

CRONE: Death and rebirth, sovereignty, inner strength

WEATHER MAGICK

Working with the Undines, the elemental spirits of water, to focus on moon lore and the ebb and flow of the tides to raise winds and cause storms, works with the chaotic forces of nature, connecting with the Sea Witch within. A Weather Witch works with the basic elements and the chaotic and unpredictable forces of nature. Weather magick can be used to influence the outcome of battle, as well as causing chaos. A Weather Witch draws to herself her power when casting spells and is able to conjure weather spells, and ones for retribution. She knows how to raise gusts of wind, to summon up lightening and drive in torrential rain, in order to blow her enemies off course. Weather magick can be used to influence the outcome of battle, as well as causing chaos.

KNOT MAGICK

Using knot magick enables one to control and generate the winds to blow you right on course, or another off. Knots hold powerful, symbolic and magickal significance. They are used as a powerful talisman and some fishermen still carry a piece of rope with three knots in it for protection against storms. Knots and knot magick are closely associated with witches, the Three Fates, in Greek mythology, weaving and knotting the threads of existence. Ancient Egyptians believed that the knot symbolised eternal life and tied a knot in their sandals called the Knot of Isis.

---

7   Monday

---

8   Tuesday
Full Moon

---

9   Wednesday
Ama Hemnmah (1947-2010) was burnt to death for confessing to be a witch in Ghana.

---

10   Thursday

---

11   Friday

KITCHEN WITCHERY

BLACKBERRY – An invasive presence and blatant disrespect of your boundaries could be making you feel uncomfortable. Neighbour disputes may be an issue for you as boundary lines are crossed, and you might be fighting for some personal space at work. Someone in your life wants more than you are willing to give, but won't take 'no' for an answer and the intrusion is becoming quite invasive of your privacy. Time to break away and free yourself from the entrapment and attachments of others, and heal from anything that is causing your dis-ease. If you permit, I shall protect you from unwanted invasion with my thorny branches. Encourage me to ramble across your garden to prevent energy vampires from crossing your threshold and if the perpetrator draws blood from my thorns, as dark and juicy as my berries, then you can be sure that justice is served.

BLACKBERRY ~ INVASIVE

Time to break free, boundaries in place.
Intruder, stalker, get out of my face!
Thorny sharp branches and berries of black,
protect from invasion to prevent attack.
This magick is worked, with harm to none.
So mote it be. There, it is done.

---

12   Saturday

---

13   Sunday

NOVEMBER

14   Monday

15   Tuesday

16   Wednesday
Third Quarter Moon.

17   Thursday

18   Friday

WITCHY RECIPE

Blackberry Jam – Can also be used in cakes, preserves and jellies.

Place a pound of the berries and a squeeze of lemon juice in a large pan and simmer until fruit is soft. Warm a pound of sugar in low oven then add fruit and stir over low heat until sugar dissolves. Now bring to the boil for about 15 minutes. Once setting point has been reached take pan off heat. Skim the scum off the top of the jam and leave to sit for 15 minutes. Pour the jam into 2 sterilised jars and seal right away. Once cooled, label and date the jars.

19   Saturday

20   Sunday

BOUNDARIES SPELL

Hold a piece of rope and elder wood as you face the direction of North at dusk under a Dark Moon and say:

Limits reached; boundaries crossed
Advantage taken; respect lost
Standing strong upon the earth
Elder dispel to rebirth.
Wrap the rope around the wood
Biding two words 'yes' and 'should'
Releasing any obligation
Banishing all exploitation
Divide and part, now draw the line
Boundaries placed; my life is mine!

Purposefully draw a line with roped wood in the ground before you. Your boundaries are now finely in place which no one can cross. So mote it be

21   Monday

22 Tuesday

Frank Hartmann (1838–1912), Occultist, Doctor, Astrologer and Theosophist.

23 Wednesday

New Moon.

24 Thursday

25 Friday

Helen Duncan (1897–1956) was the last person imprisoned under the Witchcraft Act of 1735.

26 Saturday

27 Sunday

28 Monday

29 Tuesday

30 Wednesday
First Quarter Moon · Ralph Harvey (1928–2020), Occultist, High Priest and teacher.

1 Thursday
Malleus Maleficarum was written by a catholic clergyman and endorsed the extermination of witches in 1486. This book had a strong influence on witch trials that followed.

2 Friday
Franz Bardon the Magician (1909–1958), Occultist, teacher of Hermetics.

3   Saturday
Over 123 people burnt in India for sorcery and witchcraft between 2016–19.

4   Sunday

DECEMBER
Wolf, Elder, Cold Moon

———○———

A time of quiet introspection and expectation.

In the Northern Hemisphere, Winter is a mystical artist who paints a breathless picture of landscapes adorned in jewels of sparkling frost and glistening ice. It is a time when one's breath is visible on a cold, brisk day, where trees stand stark and bare, and nature is stripped of its former glory – to its very core.

This is a season where mystery hangs in the air as dark nights draw in, enveloping the weakened, low slung sun, when the earth is steeped in deep magick and mystery, which nurtures and restores all that reside within it. A time of looking deep within and withdrawing into one's inner-cave. December is a month of hardship and discomfort, ensuring trials and tribulations for those ancestors who faced the glacial callousness of Winter, for She is a harsh taskmaster and takes no prisoners. It is a time for change, when we acknowledge and honour the cycles of death and rebirth. It's a time when hope is renewed, and like the trees of the season, we are stripped bare, naked and vulnerable as the macabre presence of the Crone shrouds us.

———○———

YULE Northern Hemisphere: 21 December

———○———

GODDESS: Cailleach (Celtic/Scottish), the Crone who rules over Winter begins to fade as the returning sun shines new promises of hope, light and a new dawn.

CRONE: Hideous queen of Winter, bearer of storms, instigator of death.

YULE

A celebration of the rebirth of the sun, from the darkness growing into the light.

Yule is the Sabbat of the Winter Solstice, the shortest day and the least productive time in nature's annual cycle. This is the longest night, of more than 12 hours of darkness as we wait for the dawn. The tradition of a mid-winter festival is ancient, which our ancestors looked forward to, through the cold barren days of December.

Yule is a celebration of the rebirth of the sun, for after the longest night, the sun will again begin to grow stronger. A sacred time of solar rebirth when we bring into our homes the yule log for the returning sun, mistletoe for fertility and holly for protection. This Sabbat represents the rebirth of light. Here, on the longest night of the year, the Goddess gives birth to the Sun God and hope for new light is reborn.

This is a time-honoured tradition when our ancestors and faeries alike would gather to welcome the return of the Sun. For at Winter Solstice the Sun appears at its weakest, having waned in strength since peaking at Summer Solstice, or Litha, six months earlier. Great cheers ring out in celebration, for on the very next Winter's morn the Sun starts its ascent steadily becoming stronger as it heads towards the Summer months once again. The birth of the Sun – the light of the world! The new king is heralded!

This time the Oak King prevails over the Holly King to bring us the light half of the year. Holly King is the overseer of holly trees, he rules the forests and woods during the Autumn and Winter after battling with the Oak King at Summer Solstice. Then they battle again at Yule when The Oak King, guardian of oak trees, wins and rules the forests and woods over the Spring and Summer. Their battle reflects the balance of the seasons. The wheel has turned. We celebrate the re-emergence of light out of darkness, bringing renewal of life and the promise of a successful future.

YULE INCANTATION

Faery folk tip toe soft,
Across the land of snow and frost,
Towards a holly tree at Yule
T'is time to cut it from its rule.
For in this battle, Oak King wins,
To lord over months to take through Spring
And in the morn turn to the Sun,
Who is born again, the light has won!
Each year the sacred wheel doth turn,
Now Yuletide's here, t'is our concern,
To celebrate with joy and mirth,
May bells ring out for 'peace on Earth'.
So place the logs upon the fire,
And make wishes of hearts' desire,
Honour the flames that warm the cool,
With blessings to one and all this Yule.

5   Monday

Pope Innocent VIII published a Papal Bull condemning witchcraft in 1484.

6   Tuesday
Dion Fortune (1890–1946), Occultist, Ceremonial Magician.

7   Wednesday

8   Thursday
Full Moon.

9   Friday

10   Saturday

11   Sunday

---

12   Monday

---

13   Tuesday

---

14   Wednesday

---

15   Thursday

Anna Franklin (1955), High Priestess, best-selling author of over 20 books on witchcraft · Amina Bint Abdulhalim beheaded in 2011 in Saudi Arabia for witchcraft.

---

16   Friday

Third Quarter Moon · In Tanzania over 40,000 people accused of witchcraft, many tried and killed between 1960 to 2000.

WITCH'S WISDOM

Like the celebrated mid-winter's Sun, it's time to make your ascent. You are rapidly growing stronger and a journey to higher heights awaits. Yule honours the return of the Sun's strength; it is a celebration of its re-birth. You too can prepare to celebrate, for your battle has been won, and you can take your deserved place next to the winning Oak King who reigns supreme at Yule, over the Holly King, until they meet again at the Solstice of Summer. So spruce yourself up, for Yule brings great news of impending rebirth, for a new way of life is just around the corner. Rebirth can come in many forms, such as heading in a new direction, promotion, a new job, new perception, empowerment or enhanced connection with the Old Ways. Whatever it is you have been asking for and visualising comes to pass when Yule arrives. So be expectant and positive as Rebirth accompanies you through to the other side, where you will emerge wiser and stronger than ever before.

INCANTATION

You waned, now growing like the Sun,
Who's born again, the light has won!
With Yule log placed upon the fire,
Rebirth delivers hearts' desire,
This magick is worked, with harm to none
So mote it be. There, it is done.

---

17   Saturday

Edith Rose Woodford-Grimes (1887-1975), one of the first adherents of English Wicca. Working partner of Gerald Gardner.

---

18   Sunday

19   Monday
Ronald Hutton (1953–), historian specialising in witchcraft, paganism and British folklore.

20   Tuesday

21   Wednesday
Yule (Winter Solstice).

22   Thursday

23   Friday
New Moon.

KITCHEN WITCHERY

ECHINACEA – When your defences are down and you're feeling low, allow me to strengthen your weakened resolve. Don't be fooled by my pretty, dainty purple petals, for I have the power to enhance your immune system. Just a couple of drops of my tincture will fortify you against the symptoms of sniffles, flu and colds, as I battle against infection on your behalf. Support is what you need as you toughen up. Just as I thrive and grow within the secure confines of an herbaceous border it is imperative that you build your defences. I will lend you my protective shield to activate and maintain your core strength and help you adjust through this period of emotional and spiritual transition. As you work with the magickal and healing properties of my coned flower I will help boost your clairvoyant and psychic abilities, and restore your energy to enhance and raise your Cone of Power when working in ritual magick.

ECHINACEA ~ FORTIFY

Infections, flu, begone, away!
I'll make sure they'll never stay
Pretty petals, cones that flower,
enhance, restore your Cone of Power
This magick is worked, with harm to none.
So mote it be. There, it is done.

24 Saturday

25 Sunday

WITCHY RECIPE

Tincture Tonic – Used as a cough medicine for colds and flu.

Fill a pint-sized jar with half a cup of either leaf and root of echinacea or dried leaf. Slowly pour boiling water over the herb to draw out the properties. Once the jar is half full of water add apple cider with the mother to the top of jar and stir. Store for 6 months shaking daily. Then strain through cheesecloth and decant into bottles and store in a dark place.

HOME SPELL

To magnetise protection and warmth in your home, face the direction of East at dawn during a New Moon phase. Hold a piece of amethyst and a bunch of lavender, and say:

Some lavender for calmness and peace.
Amethyst to create space and increase,
protection from harm at my back door.
Crystals on sills and placed on the floor
As the sun rises this very dawn
A new warmth unfurls upon sacred morn
Boundaries in place, my own sanctuary
My home is my castle 'tis where I should be.

Open the windows for fresh air to breathe new life into your home.

26   Monday

27 Tuesday

28 Wednesday

29 Thursday

30 Friday
First Quarter Moon · Maxine Sanders (1946–), High Priestess and Occultist.

31 Saturday

1 Sunday

WITCHES OF ROYALTY

JOAN OF NAVARRE, *Queen of England*
Born: c.1368 | **Died:** 10 June 1437
Accused of witchcraft

ELEANOR COBHAM, *Duchess of Gloucester*
Born: c.1400 | **Died:** 7 July 1452
Accused of witchcraft

JACQUETTA WOODVILLE, *Duchess of Bedford*
Born: c.1416 | **Died:** 30 May 1472
Accused of witchcraft

ELIZABETH WOODVILLE, *Queen of England*
Born: c.1437 | **Died:** 8 June 1492
Accused of witchcraft

Witches museums, memorials and places to visit

Arnemetia's Magical Emporium, Buxton, UK
Mother Shiptons Cave, Knarebrough, UK
Museum of Witchcraft and Magic, Boscastle, Cornwall UK
Pendle Heritage Centre, Pendle, Lancaster, UK
Museum of Witchcraft and Wizardry, Stratford on Avon, UK
Salem Witch Museum and Memorial, Salem Massachusetts, USA
Buckland Museum of Witchcraft and Magic, Cleveland, Ohio, USA
New Orleans Historic Voodoo Museum, New Orleans Louisiana, USA
Icelandic Sorcery and Witchcraft, Hólmavík, Iceland
Witches Weigh House, Oudewater, Netherlands
Magicum, Berlin Magic Museum, Berlin, Germany
Hexenmuseum Schweiz, Granichen, Switzerland
Zugarramurdi Witch Museum, Zugarramurdi, Spain

Witch Organisations

Children of Artemis
Witchcraft.org

UK Pagan Federation
Paganfed.org

Notes

Witchy Fact

A Canadian Law states that to pretend to practice witchcraft is illegal.
But practising the craft for real is recognised as legit!

Notes